PICTURE GUIDE TO
TREE LEAVES

PICTURE GUIDE
TO
TREE LEAVES

RAYMOND WIGGERS

FRANKLIN WATTS
NEW YORK / LONDON / TORONTO
SYDNEY
1991
A FIRST BOOK

Cover photograph courtesy of Donald J. Leopold

All photographs courtesy of Donald J. Leopold except:
Animals Animals/Earth Scenes: p. 47 top right (B. G. Murray Jr.);
Photo Researchers Inc.: pp. 47 top left (H. F. Flanders),
47 bottom (Ken Brate), 57 (Rod Planck), 58 (Farrell Grehan).

Library of Congress Cataloging-in-Publication Data

Wiggers, Raymond.
Picture guide to tree leaves / by Raymond Wiggers.
p.   cm. — (A First book)
Includes bibliographical references and index.
Summary: Demonstrates, through the use of photographs, how
different kinds of trees can be identified.
ISBN 0-531-20025-6
1. Trees—Identification—Juvenile literature.   2. Leaves—
Identification—Juvenile literature.   3. Trees—United States—
Identification—Juvenile literature.   4. Leaves—United States—
Identification—Juvenile literature.   [1. Trees—Identification.
2. Leaves—Identification.]   I. Title.   II. Series.
QK477.2.I6W54   1991
582.16—dc20   90-47859 CIP   AC

CONTENTS

HOW TREES ARE IDENTIFIED

THE TWO MAIN KINDS OF TREES

Trees can be divided into two main groups. The first group is the more ancient—it appeared roughly 200 million years ago. In other words, plants of this group were growing when the earliest dinosaurs walked the earth. The trees of this group are called *conifers* (CON-if-ers), or cone-bearers. You have only to think of a pine cone to see that pine trees are a good example of this group. One of the best ways to identify a conifer is by its needlelike leaves, such as those found on Christmas trees.

Besides pines, such trees as spruces and the gigantic redwoods of California are conifers. In fact, the redwoods are the largest living things in the world. Other conifers have set another kind of record by being some of the oldest living things. For instance, some pines still living today sprouted from their seeds thousands of years ago!

The second main group are the *broad-leaved trees*. As the name suggests, their leaves are broader than the needles found on conifers. Oaks and maples are good examples of this second group. While broad-leaved trees appeared millions of years before human beings, they are still the newcomers of the plant world. Their history stretches back only to the final part of the Age of Dinosaurs. They've been very successful, however, and are now far more numerous than other kinds of trees.

THE TREE'S THREE PARTS

Every tree has three basic parts. Starting below ground, the *roots* anchor the tree in the soil and gather water and food (nutrients) from it. The *trunk* is the tree's vertical support. The water and nutrients travel up the trunk to the *crown*, which is the tree's leaf-bearing branches. The leaves are the most amazing part of the whole tree—here the water and nutrients are turned into food for use by the whole plant. The leaves do this by using sunlight in a complicated process known as photosynthesis.

HOW TO IDENTIFY TREES

There are a number of things to look for when you want to identify a tree. The *leaves* are often a good way to identify a tree, but of course this method won't work in fall or wintertime if the tree has shed its foliage. One method that does work in winter is to check a tree's *buds*. Buds are the small bumps on the ends of twigs where next year's leaves and flowers will emerge. Each type of tree has buds of a certain size and shape.

Another way to identify a tree is to look at its *bark*. This can be helpful even though a tree's bark often changes as the tree gets older. Finally, a particular type of tree can sometimes be recognized by its overall shape, or *habit*. Maple trees, for instance, often look lollipop-shaped from a distance, while some poplars have a tall, narrow habit.

There is one thing you should keep in mind when you begin identifying the trees shown in this book. Trees are complex living beings. As you'll see when you walk through a park or a forest, each tree has its own shape, size, and other traits. Even trees of the same variety differ from each other to some degree. Don't be discouraged. Before long you will be able to recognize these differences. Have fun!

PART ONE

THE CONIFERS
(AND A RELATIVE)

THE PINES

Pines are some of the most common cone-bearing trees. They can be recognized by their narrow green needles and their bark, which is often rough and scaly. If you look at how the needles are connected to their stems, you'll see that they're attached at the bottom and arranged in little bundles. Some kinds of pines have five needles in each bundle, and some have only two or three.

Another way you can identify pines is to examine their cones. Some cones are long and skinny, and some are short and round; some have prickles on them, and some don't.

There are many types of pines native to the United States. For example, the **eastern white pine** and the **red pine** are characteristic of the northeastern states, and the **loblolly pine** and **longleaf pine** are found in the South. **Pinyon** pines are native to the Southwest, and the **lodgepole pine** and **ponderosa pine** grow in the West, from the Rocky Mountains to the Pacific coast.

If you look in parks or private yards you will often find other types of pine trees, too. These are descendants of trees that were brought to America from other countries. The **Scots pine** and **Austrian pine** have been planted here for many decades. A more recent arrival is the stately **Himalayan pine**, which has needles that droop downward from its branches, as well as cones coated with sticky resin.

loblolly pine
needles 5″–10″ long,
3 needles per cluster

SPRUCES AND TRUE FIRS

Next to the pines, the spruces and true firs are some of the most frequently found conifers. They have a distinctive "Christmas tree" shape that often sets them apart from pine trees.

The needles of spruces and firs are different, too. Instead of being attached in little bundles, the way pine needles are, they are attached separately, one by one, to the twigs. The needles of spruces have pointed tips, while those on true firs have rounded tips.

Spruces can also be distinguished from true firs by their cones. Spruce cones hang down from the branches; the cones of true firs stick up.

Several types of spruces are native to the United States. In the West, the **Colorado spruce** and the **Engelmann spruce** are found in the Rocky Mountain states, and the **Sitka spruce** is found in the Pacific Northwest. In the Northeast, the **red spruce** and **black spruce** are common. The magnificent **Norway spruce**, introduced from Europe, is also frequently seen in yards and parks.

The most common true fir is the **balsam fir**, which grows in the northern part of our country.

Colorado spruce
needles about 1″ long

balsam fir
needles $3/8″$–$1 1/4″$ long

Canadian hemlock
needles $^5/_{16}"-^9/_{16}"$ long

Douglas fir
needles $1"-1^1/_2"$ long

CANADIAN HEMLOCK AND DOUGLAS FIR

The **Douglas fir** and the **Canadian hemlock** resemble the spruces and true firs, but if you look closely you can see some important differences. The cones of the Canadian hemlock are really small—only $^1/_2$ inch (1.3 cm) or a little longer—and its needles have two white bands on their undersides.

Unlike the cones of true firs, Douglas fir cones hang *down* from the branches. These cones are very distinctive—they have long spikes called *bracts* that stick out from them.

The Douglas fir is native to the American West, though it has been planted in many other places. The Canadian hemlock can be found mainly in our northern states. As its name suggests, it is also found in Canada.

18

LARCHES AND THE BALD CYPRESS

These trees are unusual for conifers. Most cone-bearing trees are *evergreen*—they keep their needles throughout the winter. But **larches** and the **bald cypress** drop their needles each fall and have bare branches till the following spring.

One kind of larch tree, usually called **tamarack**, is native to the northern United States. The **European larch** is also found growing in some American city parks. Both trees have needles attached to their stems in clusters. The cones of the tamarack are much smaller than those of the European larch.

The bald cypress is found in swamps and other wet ground in the American South. Its cones look like little round balls, and its needles resemble those of the Canadian hemlock. Often the bald cypress has knobby growths around the base of the trunk. These growths are called *knees*.

tamarack
needles ³/₈″–1″ long

bald cypress
needles ¹/₄″–⁷/₈″ long

19

RED CEDAR AND ARBORVITAE

These two evergreen trees may be hard to tell apart at first. Still, if you look closely you will notice that the **red cedar** has small blue "berries" (actually soft-skinned cones) while the **arborvitae** (ARE-burr VIE-tee) has tiny woody cones. Also, the needles of the arborvitae are arranged in flat sprays—they almost look like they've been pressed. On the other hand, the red cedar has two types of needles.

The red cedar and the arborvitae are both native to the eastern United States, and they can be found both in the wild and in parks and yards.

red cedar
leaves $1/16''$–$3/4''$ long

arborvitae
leaves $1/16''$–$1/8''$ long

gingko
leaves 3"–4"

THE GINKGO

If a dinosaur suddenly were to appear in our own times, the ginkgo tree would be one of the few things it would recognize. This unusual tree has been around for many millions of years— much longer than most other living things.

The ginkgo's fan-shaped leaves are unique. If you look closely at the leaves you'll notice they have tiny veins that run from the base of the stem to the outer edge. Many trees have larger veins that run down the middle of their leaves, but ginkgo veins are all the same size.

Unlike most of the conifers, which are its distant relatives, the ginkgo sheds its leaves each fall and then grows new ones the following spring. The new leaves emerge from peglike spurs on the branches.

The ginkgo is often called a "living fossil" because of its amazing survival record. It was widespread during the age of the dinosaurs, but by the time human beings came along, this grand old veteran of the plant kingdom was nearly extinct. In fact, it could only be found growing in one area of China. Fortunately, people recognized its worth and beauty, and today it can be found in parks and along city streets around the globe.

One warning about the ginkgo: the female trees bear fruit that look like green or yellow plums. These fruits are sticky and slippery, and they smell very bad. Don't try to handle or eat them!

PART TWO

THE BROAD-LEAVED TREES

OAKS

We begin our survey of broad-leaved trees with the oaks. When people think of oaks they usually think of giant, sturdy trees that live for hundreds of years. Oaks actually come in all sizes— some never grow larger than garden shrubs.

The leaves of oak trees vary a great deal. Some, like those of the **live oak**, have smooth edges; others, like those of the **pin oak**, are deeply notched and have projections called *lobes*. But there's one thing all oaks have in common: they all produce fruit called *acorns*.

America is home to many kinds of oak trees. In the northeastern states, the **northern red oak**, the **black oak**, and the **pin oak** are especially common. The South is home to the majestic, spreading **live oak**, as well as to the **southern red oak** and **willow oak**. The **white oak** can be found all the way from New England to eastern Texas.

The **Arizona white oak** and **Emory oak** are native to the American Southwest, and nearer the Pacific coast one finds the **California black oak** and **canyon live oak**

The leaves and acorns may be the easiest way to identify oaks in the summer and fall, but in winter the buds on oak twigs are another method of telling oaks from other trees. Look at the tips of oak branches, and you'll see clusters of several little buds. Most other trees have only one bud on each stem tip.

southern red oak
leaves 4″–10″ long

tanbark oak
leaves 2"–5" long

American beech
leaves 1"–5" long

THE TANBARK OAK AND THE BEECHES

These trees are relatives of the oaks. The **tanbark oak**, a native of California and Oregon, produces acorns just as the true oaks do. In contrast, the beeches have small, triangle-shaped nuts inside spiny husks.

The **American beech** grows wild in the eastern half of the United States. Its leaves have pointed tips and small teeth along the edges. The **European beech** is also found in America, especially in city parks. Its leaves are somewhat smaller and rounder. The leaves of the tanbark oak are dark green, leathery, and evergreen.

BIRCHES

One of the most distinctive trees in North America is the **paper birch**, with its white, peeling bark. It is just one of several birches native to this continent.

The leaves of all the birches are fringed with tiny teeth. In spring, birch trees produce long dangling flowers called *catkins*.

The paper birch is well adapted to life in a cold climate, and it grows wild in our northernmost states. The **water birch**, a native of the West, has brown bark; it resembles the **river birch**, a tree with pink, brown, or black bark that grows in the Midwest and the East. In the Northeast you can find the silver-barked **yellow birch** as well as the brown- or black-barked **sweet birch**.

In addition to these native birches, the **European white birch** is often planted in parks and gardens. It resembles our paper birch, but its leaves are smaller and its white bark doesn't peel as readily.

gray birch
leaves 1"–4" long

THE AMERICAN HORNBEAM AND
EASTERN HOP HORNBEAM

These two trees are relatives of the birches. They are both found in the eastern half of the United States, and both have leaves with toothed edges. In fact, the leaves are so similar that it's hard to tell the two apart.

Fortunately the **American hornbeam** and the **Eastern hop hornbeam** do differ in other ways. Both have dangling catkins for flowers, but their fruits are different. The American hornbeam fruit looks like bunches of small angel wings. The eastern hop hornbeam has pods that almost look like small pine cones.

The bark of the two trees is a giveaway, too. The American hornbeam has smooth, steel-gray bark that often suggests flexed muscles. In contrast, eastern hop hornbeam bark is reddish brown, and it peels in little strips.

American hornbeam
leaves 1"–5" long

Eastern hop hornbeam
leaves 1"–5" long

black willow
leaves 1"–6" long

quaking aspen
leaves 2"–3" long

WILLOWS, POPLARS, AND ASPENS

Willow trees are often found growing near streams and rivers. There are several kinds of tree-sized willows native to North America—among them are the **black willow**, **Pacific willow**, and **peachleaf willow**. In addition, imported varieties such as the **weeping willow** are now very common in America. Generally, willow leaves are long and narrow, with tiny teeth on their edges.

Poplars and aspens are close relatives of willows, but their leaves are rounder or more wedge-shaped. The most common of the poplars are the **cottonwoods**, which grow across much of the United States. Two aspens are found in the cooler parts of our country: the **quaking aspen**, which grows in the Rockies and in most of our northern states; and the **bigtooth aspen**, which is confined to north-central and northeastern states.

29

ELMS, THE HACKBERRY, AND THE SUGARBERRY

Elm trees can be identified by their jagged, double-toothed leaves and the small, waferlike fruit that are produced in great numbers. If you take a closer look at the leaves, you'll see their bases are uneven—one side goes further down the stem than the other.

The most famous and most stately elm is the **American elm** One of the most beautiful things about this magnificent tree is its graceful vase-shaped habit (overall shape). The American elm once shaded the streets of many towns across the country, but now it is less common. The Dutch elm disease has killed thousands of American elms in the past fifty years. There is still no reliable cure for this disease.

The **winged elm** is found in the South. It has smaller leaves and conspicuous twigs with corky wings on them. The disease-resistant **Chinese elm** is an import from the Far East. It has small leaves—sometimes an inch (2.5 cm) or less in length.

The **hackberry** and the **sugarberry** are relatives of the elms. The sugarberry, a native of the South, has tapered, smooth-edged leaves. The hackberry, found in the Northeast and the Midwest, has leaves with small teeth and a somewhat curved tip.

American elm
leaves 2″–6″ long

hackberry
leaves 3″–7″ long

MAGNOLIAS AND THE TULIP TREE

The big white or pinkish flowers of magnolia trees are a sure sign of spring, but it isn't hard to identify magnolias in the winter, either. Look for their big, fuzzy buds that resemble pussy willows. (Incidentally, pussy willows are true, shrub-sized willows—don't confuse them with the magnolias!)

Most of our native magnolias—such as the **sweetbay** and the **umbrella**, **bigleaf**, and **southern magnolias**—grow in the wild in the Southeast, but another type of magnolia, the **cucumber tree**, can be found as far north as Pennsylvania. Magnolia leaves have smooth edges—the leaves of the umbrella and bigleaf magnolias can be over a foot and a half long!

Among the imported magnolias, the **saucer magnolia** and **star magnolia** are especially common. They are quite hardy and can be found in New England and other northern states.

The magnificent **tulip tree** is a close relative of the magnolias. It gets its name from its green and orange-yellow tulip-shaped flowers. The tulip tree grows to great size with a tall, straight trunk. It is native to much of the eastern United States.

cucumber tree (magnolia)
leaves 4"–7" long

yellow poplar ("tulip tree")
leaves 6"–10" long

MAPLES

It would be hard to imagine autumn without maple trees. Their bright fall colors stand out vividly among the more subdued colors of oaks and other trees. Maples are important to us for other reasons, too. They are excellent shade trees for parks and homes, and one kind of maple tree provides maple syrup.

There are a number of maples native to the United States. The **red maple** grows in much of the eastern half of our country. Its leaves turn bright red in fall. The **sugar maple**, the chief source of the highly prized sugar sap, is found in the Northeast. It puts on a brilliant show in autumn, too: its leaves turn orange, flame pink, or bright yellow.

The **silver maple**, also native to the East, has deeply-cut leaves. The **bigleaf maple** of the Pacific coast is well named because its leaves can measure a foot across. The **box elder** is unusual for another reason; its leaves are cut into three or more distinct parts called *leaflets*. It grows near creeks, rivers, and lakes across most of the country.

Among the maples originally from overseas, two kinds are often planted here as shade trees. The **sycamore maple** is a common sight in city parks in the East. (Make sure that you don't confuse it with the true sycamore tree.) The extremely common **Norway maple** has leaves very similar to the sugar maple's. Still, it isn't hard to tell the two maples apart. A sugar maple leaf, when carefully removed from its branch, bleeds clear sap from its stem. In contrast, the Norway maple has a milky white sap.

bigleaf maple
leaves 8″–12″

sugar maple
leaves 2″–10″ long

THE SWEET GUM AND WITCH HAZEL

These two trees are fairly close relatives of one another, but you probably won't be able to detect many family resemblances. The **sweet gum** grows to be a big shade tree; the **witch hazel** is a small tree at best, rarely growing taller than 25 feet (8 m).

Still, both trees are easy to identify. The sweet gum, a native of the warmer parts of the American East and Midwest, has distinctive star-shaped leaves with five or seven pointed lobes. Its twigs often have corky wings. The sweet gum's flowers are hard to see, but the fruit—balls with little spikes or horns—can't be missed. One of the best things about the sweet gum is the color display it puts on in fall. Its leaves can vary from bright yellow to red to purple.

The witch hazel grows throughout most of the eastern half of our country. Its unusual leaves have wavy margins and uneven bases. But the most surprising thing about the witch hazel is the time it chooses to flower. Most trees and other plants bloom in spring or summer, but the witch hazel doesn't produce its wispy yellow flowers until autumn or early winter. If you're lucky, you may walk through a snowy forest in December and see a witch hazel pretending it's spring!

sweet gum
leaves 5″–8″ long

witch hazel
leaves 2″–7″ long

sassafras
leaves 2"–7" long

SASSAFRAS, REDBAY, AND CALIFORNIA LAUREL

These three small trees of the laurel family have a special way of being identified. When you crush their leaves they release a pleasant, spicy smell.

The sassafras, a native of the eastern states both north and south, has very distinctive leaves that come in three different shapes: with three lobes, two lobes, or no lobes at all. They turn bright red or yellow in fall.

The leaves of the redbay and the California laurel are leathery and evergreen. They have smooth edges with no lobes. Redbay is found in our southern states along the Atlantic and Gulf coasts. The California laurel grows in the Pacific coast area.

redbay
leaves 3″–6″ long

California laurel
leaves 2″–5″ long

American sycamore
leaves 6″–10″ long

THE SYCAMORE AND THE LONDON PLANE TREE

At first glance the **sycamore** and the **London plane tree** are easy to confuse with maples. Their leaves have a maple-leaf shape. But actually they're members of a different plant family altogether. This becomes clearer when you look at the unusual, patchy bark of the London plane and the sycamore. The individual patches of bark can be white, brown, orange, or even a light green. And instead of the maples' winged fruit, the sycamore and the London plane have seed balls that hang down on slender stems.

Telling these two trees apart can be difficult. One of the best identification clues is where the trees grow. The sycamore (which shouldn't be confused with the sycamore maple) is an American native most often found growing in the woods of the East and the Midwest. Chances are you'll find the London plane, originally from the Old World, planted in parks and along city streets, especially on the East Coast.

THE AILANTHUS

The tree called the ailanthus (eye-LAN-thus) is sometimes also known as the tree of heaven. Despite that name, it grows in places that aren't exactly heavenly, such as abandoned lots, roadsides, alleyways, and even small cracks in city sidewalks!

The people who first brought the ailanthus from its original home in China probably had no idea that it would thrive on its own in so many American cities. As it turns out, it is extremely tolerant of pollution and other adverse conditions. Ailanthus trees are capable of producing thousands of seeds each year, so the species spreads rapidly. Because of this, the ailanthus is often called a "weed tree." But we should be thankful it brings much-needed shade and greenery to otherwise bleak places.

Ailanthus leaves are composed of many pointed leaflets. The bases of the leaflets have uneven sides. When ripe, ailanthus seeds are brown and papery, and they hang in large bunches until they are dispersed by squirrels or the wind.

ailanthus
leaflets 2"–4" long

CRAB APPLES AND HAWTHORNS

These trees are members of one of the largest plant families, the Rose Family. As you might expect from these relatives of the garden rose, the **crab apple** and the **hawthorn** are highly prized for their flowers, which are small but numerous.

Both crab apples and hawthorns come in many different varieties, and most were specially developed or brought from other countries. Hawthorn and crab apple flowers are white, pink, or red, and have five small petals. The fruits of the crab apples resemble common cultivated apples, but they are much smaller. Hawthorn fruits are similar, but they are often covered with small dots.

The best way to tell a crab apple tree from a hawthorn is to check the twigs. Hawthorns have long, sharp spines (be careful!); crab apples have shorter, blunter spurs, or no spurs at all.

crab apple
leaves 1"–4" long

"Winter king" hawthorn
leaves 2"–4" long

black cherry
leaves 2″–6″ long

common pear
leaves 1″–3″ long

CHERRY AND PEAR TREES

Here are two more well-known members of the rose family. Like the trees on the preceding page, cherry and pear trees have flowers with five petals. Their blooms are usually white or pink.

Cherry trees vary in size and showiness, from small and beautiful ornamental varieties, such as the **Japanese Kwanzan cherry**, to the larger native **black cherry**, which grows in the eastern half of the United States.

One type of pear tree is now common in many American cities. The **Callery** (or **Bradford**) **pear** is a tough import from China that has been planted extensively along busy streets. Its beautiful white spring flowers and its leathery dark green leaves provide a welcome change from long stretches of concrete roadways, sidewalks, and buildings.

43

BASSWOODS AND THE LITTLE-LEAF LINDEN

The **basswoods** are linden trees native to the United States. Like their close European relative, the **little-leaf linden**, the basswoods produce fragrant yellowish-white flowers in early summer. In winter you can identify basswoods and the little-leaf linden by their red or brown buds that often resemble tiny mittens.

These trees have very characteristic leaves with sawtooth edges and unequal bases. In addition, you can identify this group by the long, strap-shaped coverings that shield their flower and fruit stems. These coverings are called *bracts*. Bracts are parts of plants that originally were leaves. In the course of many generations they gradually evolved into other shapes or sizes, to serve other functions.

The **American basswood** found in the Northeast and in the northern Midwest; it has big leaves that measure 6 inches (15 cm) or longer. The **white, Carolina** and **Florida basswoods** grow farther south. The white basswood is sometimes called the beetree because of the way it attracts swarms of bees when it is in full bloom.

The best place to find the little-leaf linden in America is in cities, where it has been planted extensively as a street tree. As its name implies, this tree has smaller leaves—only about two inches (5 cm) long.

American basswood
leaves 5″–10″ long

PALOVERDES, ACACIAS, AND MESQUITES

The American Southwest is the home of these three tree types, though one kind of acacia also grows in wild places along the Gulf Coast and in Florida. All are members of the Legume (LEG-yoom) Family. This large plant family includes peas, beans, indigo, and many other familiar plants. The legumes can be identified by their characteristic seed pods.

Acacia seed pods may be long or short, and straight or twisted, depending on the exact kind of tree. The flowers that come before the seed pods are yellow and ball- or candle-shaped. In contrast **mesquite** flowers resemble white spikes, and their seed pods are long with rounded bumps. The leaves of both the acacias and mesquites are composed of many tiny leaflets.

Paloverde trees are remarkable because their leaves (also composed of tiny leaflets) are very small. Their yellow flowers have five distinct petals.

The twigs and branches of acacias, mesquites, and paloverdes are armed with sharp spines.

sweet acacia
leaflets ¹/₄″ long

paloverde
leaflets ¹/₄″ long

honey mesquite
leaflets 1″–2″ long

LOCUSTS, THE REDBUD, AND THE KENTUCKY COFFEE TREE

These are some other notable Legume Family trees. All but one have leaves subdivided into small leaflets. The one exception is the **redbud**, which is native to almost the entire eastern United States. Its leaves are simple and heart shaped. In spring the redbud lives up to its name by producing pink or reddish flowers that seem to cover the branches.

The **black locust** and the **honey locust**, now widely planted elsewhere, were also originally from the eastern half of our country. The black locust produces dangling white flowers and pods about four inches (10 cm) in length. The honey locust has insignificant greenish flowers that turn into curved pods that can be over a foot (30.5 cm) long. In the wild, both trees are armed with thorns (though a commonly planted variety of honey locust is thornless).

The **Kentucky coffee tree** gets its name from the fact that early American settlers used its seeds as a substitute for real coffee. Its flowers are hard to see, but the wide, brownish seed pods that come from them are a good identification tool.

redbud
leaves 2″–6″ long

black locust
leaflets 1″–2″ long

Kentucky coffee tree
leaflets 2″–3″ long

Pacific madrona
leaves 3"–6" long

THE MADRONA

The **madrona**, a Pacific coast tree, grows in the wild from Canada all the way to southern California. It can reach a height of 100 feet (3 m), but most specimens are considerably smaller than that. Its leaves are evergreen and somewhat leathery.

The madrona has bark that peels to reveal pink, orange, or greenish wood. It produces clusters of small white flowers shaped like little bells. The fruits look like red or reddish orange berries.

ASH TREES

There are several different kinds of ash trees in North America, and some are so similar to one another that even experts have trouble telling them apart!

The most common members of this group are the **white ash** and the **green ash**, which inhabit the forests of the eastern half of the United States. (They are also planted in cities and towns across the country.) In common with most other ash trees, they have leaves composed of seven or more pointed leaflets.

Ash trees can be easily identified by their single-winged seeds and their gray, handsomely ridged bark. If you look closely you'll notice that the ridges often form narrow, diamond-shaped patterns.

white ash
leaflets 3"–5" long

51

TREE-SIZED DOGWOODS AND THE TUPELO

There are several types of dogwoods native to North America, but most are shrubs. The **flowering dogwood** reaches tree size, though, and it can be found planted in yards and also growing wild in the woodlands of the eastern United States. Actually, all dogwoods flower, but the flowering dogwood got its name by having especially showy blooms. Four large, white petal-like bracts surround each small flower cluster. If you look closely at these bracts, you'll see that they're notched at their tips. In winter this small tree is easy to recognize, too: look for its unusual button-shaped buds.

The **Pacific dogwood** resembles the flowering dogwood, but it has four to six flower bracts that are not notched. This tree can be found from Washington State to southern California. The **Kousa dogwood** is an Asian relative that has four sharply pointed flower bracts. The Kousa dogwood has been planted in America in many parks and gardens.

The **tupelo** is a relative of the dogwoods. Sometimes also called the **sour gum** or **black gum**, it is native to the eastern third of the United States, where it prefers streambanks and other places with damp soil. The tupelo's greenish flowers aren't easy to see, but the dark blue fruit is a helpful identification tool. Tupelo leaves turn bright red in the fall.

dogwood
leaves 2″–5″ long

tupelo
leaves 3″–6″ long

catalpa
leaves 6"–13" long

THE CATALPAS

Two types of **catalpa** trees, the northern and the southern, are native to the United States. While catalpas are easy to distinguish from other trees, it is often difficult to figure out which particular kind of catalpa you're looking at. Both types have large, woolly, heart-shaped leaves, clusters of bell-shaped flowers, and long, dangling seed pods.

The catalpas are restricted to small areas in the wild, but they are a common sight in parks and yards.

WALNUTS AND HICKORIES

Walnut and hickory trees are identified by their leaves (they are composed of many leaflets) and their fruit, which consist of nuts inside protective husks.

The **black walnut** and the **butternut** are the most common walnut trees. They are native to the eastern United States. Among the most familiar hickories are the **shagbark** (with its coarse, peeling bark) and the **pecan**, famous for its highly prized nut and its impressive size. Hickories are most frequently found in the eastern states.

black walnut
leaflets 2″–3″ long

shagbark hickory
leaflets up to 5″ long

BUCKEYES AND THE HORSE CHESTNUT

Buckeyes are American trees that can be identified by their distinctive leaves, which have five leaflets attached at a central point of the stem. They also have upright, candlelike flowers and large, shiny brown seeds enclosed in husks.

The **Ohio buckeye** and **yellow buckeye** are natives of eastern states and have yellow flowers. The **California buckeye** of the Far West has white or pinkish flowers.

The **horse chestnut**, originally from the Old World, is a close relative of the buckeyes. It is often found in American parks and yards, where its white flowers are a dramatic sight in springtime. Horse chestnut seed husks are covered with spiny prickles.

Ohio buckeye
leaflets 3"–5" long

horse chestnut
leaflets 3"–7" long

yucca
leaves 6"–12" long

YUCCAS

A striking native of the American Southwest desert is the **Joshua tree yucca**. Unlike cactus plants, the Joshua tree has long spear-shaped leaves that grow in clusters atop the plant's stems. The **aloe yucca**, a smaller relative of the Joshua tree, grows along the Gulf and Atlantic coasts as far north as the Carolinas. Yuccas produce great spikes of white flowers that rise high above the leaves.

palm
leaves usually
several feet long

PALM TREES

It's hard to think of faraway, tropical lands without thinking of palm trees. But the United States boasts a number of native palms, including the **palmettos** of the Gulf Coast, the **Florida royal palm**, and the **California Washingtonia**

Other palms, originally from other places, have been introduced into the warmer regions of the United States, too. Two well-known examples of these introduced types are the **date palm** and the **coconut palm**

Palm trees are unique in appearance, with single stems that do not keep thickening with age the way those of other trees do. The older leaves of these plants die back to reveal long, slender, and often slanting trunks that give palms their stately, if mop-headed, look.

GLOSSARY

ACORN: The fruit of oaks and tanbark oaks. An acorn is made up of a nut enclosed in a scaly cup.

BARK: The outer covering of a tree's trunk and branches.

BRACT: An attachment to a flower stem or cone that is shaped like a strap, spike, or leaf.

BROAD-LEAVED TREE: A tree that has leaves that are broader than needles. Broad-leaved trees include oaks, maples, willows, lindens, and many others.

BUD: The place on a plant's twig or stem where leaves or flowers will emerge during the next growing season. Buds are often covered with small protective scales.

CATKIN: A long cluster of tiny flowers found on oaks, birches, poplars, willows, and other trees.

CONE: A woody "seed container" found on pines, hemlocks, spruces, and many other needle-leaved trees.

CONIFER: A cone-bearing plant.

CROWN: The part of a tree that is made up of its leaf-bearing branches.

EVERGREEN: A plant, such as a pine or spruce, that keeps its leaves throughout the year.

FLOWER: The reproductive part of a plant that produces fruit.

FRUIT: A "seed container" that develops from a flower. Most broad-leaved trees produce fruit. Examples: acorns (oak), winged seeds (maple), berries (hackberry), pods (catalpa and honey locust), and of course cherries, apples, and pears.

HABIT: The overall shape of a tree, seen from a small distance.

KNEE: A knobby bump found at the base of bald cypress trees.

LEAF: The green "food factory" of a plant, where sunlight is used to help make the plant's food supplies.

LEAFLET: A smaller, separate section of a leaf. Sometimes leaflets are mistaken for entire leaves. Examples of trees with leaves divided into leaflets: acacia, honey locust, ash, buckeye.

LEGUME: A plant that is a member of the Pea Family. Legume trees include redbud, Kentucky coffee tree, Japanese pagoda tree, acacia, mesquite, and many others.

LIVING FOSSIL: A type of tree that has survived unchanged for many millions of years. The ginkgo is the best-known living fossil; its prehistoric relatives shaded the earliest dinosaurs!

LOBE: A large bump or projection on a leaf. Examples of trees with lobed leaves: maples, oaks, sassafras, sycamore.

NEEDLE: A very narrow leaf found on most cone-bearing plants. Examples: pine needles and spruce needles.

ROOTS: The underground portion of a plant. Roots anchor the plant in the soil and also absorb the water and nutrients the plant needs to make food.

SHRUB: A woody plant with more than one main stem. Shrubs are usually less than 15 feet (4.6m) tall.

TREE: A woody plant that is more than 15 feet tall when it is fully grown. Trees also usually have one main trunk.

TRUNK: The main stem of a tree. It transports water, nutrients, and food to other parts of the tree. It is also the tree's vertical support.

INDEX

ABOUT THE AUTHOR

Raymond Wiggers is the owner of North Star Plant Care in Alstead Center, New Hampshire. He holds a bachelor of science degree from Purdue University. He has also been a naval officer, public-radio classical-music announcer, community-garden planner and horticulturist, and a tree-care instructor. This is his first published book.